BENEATH PEARL HARBOR

YOUNG READER EDITION

BY NAOMI S. BLINICK

PHOTOGRAPHS BY BRETT T. SEYMOUR

ADDITIONAL CONTRIBUTIONS BY EMILY PRUETT

BEST PUBLISHING COMPANY
BPC KIDS™

ISBN: 978-1-947239-10-4
Library of Congress Control Number: 2018943666

Version 1.0

Printed and bound in the United States of America.

Best Publishing Company
631 US Highway 1, Suite 307
North Palm Beach, FL 33408

The opinions expressed in this work are those of the authors and do not reflect the opinions of Best
Publishing Company or its editors.

The views expressed in this work are those of the individual authors and do not necessarily represent
any position, official or otherwise, of the National Park Service or the United States of America.

Information contained in this work has been obtained by Best Publishing Company and the authors
from sources believed to be reliable. However, neither Best Publishing Company nor its authors guar-
antees the accuracy or completeness of any information published herein, and neither Best Publishing
Company nor its authors shall be responsible for any errors, omissions, or claims for damages, including
exemplary damages, arising out of use, inability to use, or with regard to the accuracy or sufficiency of
the information contained in this publication.

Diving is an activity that has inherent risks. All persons who wish to engage in diving activities must
receive professional instruction. The authors, publisher, and any other party associated with production
of this book does not accept responsibility for any accident or injury resulting from diving.

Civilian diving on USS *Arizona* or USS *Utah* is strictly prohibited. Pearl Harbor is an active U.S. Navy base
and diving is conducted solely for government-approved purposes.

The USS *Arizona* is the most well-known battleship sunk during the Japanese attack on Pearl Harbor, Hawaii, on December 7, 1941. This unprovoked attack on a U.S. Navy base pushed the United States into World War II.

This book is about Pearl Harbor and the final resting place of the USS *Arizona*. It is a place that changed the course of history and one of the most popular locations to visit in Hawaii. Have you ever wondered what it looks like under the waters of Pearl Harbor? In this book, you can explore the USS *Arizona* alongside National Park Service scuba divers, who use diving as a tool to study and preserve the ship. The goal of this book is to share one of the most historic shipwrecks of all time and show you what the wreck looked like before and after the events of December 7, 1941.

Located on the **stern** of the USS *Arizona*, this open hatch with stairs once descended to the captain's cabin and stateroom on the second deck. Today it leads into 75 years of **sediment** buildup with only enough room for fish to access the ship's interior.

TABLE OF CONTENTS

USS *Arizona* underway in the East River heading to the New York Naval Yard with the Brooklyn Bridge and Manhattan skyline in the background. December 26, 1916.

GLOSSARY

Here are some helpful definitions of words that may be new to you in this book. You will see them in **bold** throughout the text. Many of these words have more complex meanings, but for simplicity they are explained as they relate to the USS *Arizona*.

archaeologist. A scientist who studies archaeology.

archaeology. The study of human history through digging up or studying objects like tools, buildings, ships, pottery, and jewelry.

archive. A collection of records, such as books, films, or audio recordings, kept to help people learn about a time, place, person, or group.

artifact. An object made or used by humans in the past.

barbette. A heavily armored vertical tube that supports a gun turret (see turret). On the USS *Arizona*, several of the barbettes are open and look like big holes in the deck from above.

battleship. A large military ship that has large guns and heavy armor.

bow. The front part of a boat or ship.

Bunker-C oil. The type of fuel oil battleships were filled with at the time of the Pearl Harbor attack, including the USS *Arizona*. It is this oil that still leaks today. Unlike gasoline, Bunker-C is very thick and evaporates slowly.

catapult. A machine for launching planes from the deck of a ship.

commission. The act of assigning a military ship to active service. This is usually done by a high-ranking military official during a ceremony after the ship is built.

coral bleaching. Corals will turn white from the stress of high water temperatures. They may recover and turn back to their natural color or they may die, turning brown and becoming covered in algae.

corrode. Slowly being worn away or weakened by a chemical process. Rust is a type of corrosion.

current. The flow of water or air in one direction.

cutwater. The forward edge of a ship.

decade. A time period of ten years.

deck. The floor on a ship or boat.

deteriorate. To break down and weaken.

encrusting marine life. Sea animals that live in one place and create a thick covering over the seafloor or other surface. Examples include corals and sponges.

estimate. An educated guess.

exoskeleton. A protective external covering in an animal without a backbone. A crab shell is an exoskeleton.

Great Depression. The decade of the 1930s in America when there was extreme economic hardship.

half-staff. Flying a flag below the top of its mast as a sign of respect for a person or people who have died.

historic site. A place that is important in history, such as a battlefield, shipwreck, or building.

honor guard. A group of people in the uniform of their organization, such as the military, police, or the National Park Service, present at funerals. They usually carry a flag of their country and other flags of the organization.

hull. The frame and outer shell of a ship or boat, including the bottom, sides, and deck.

iconic. A person or thing that is greatly respected and admired.

inter. Another word for burial. Used when referring to the burial of USS *Arizona* survivors in the ship.

inventory. A complete list of things in a specific place.

keel. A long piece of wood or metal that runs along the entire bottom of a boat or ship. The keel gives the ship stability.

memorial. A building, statue, or ceremony to honor a past event, a dead person, or people.

modernize. To make something old newer and bring it up-to-date.

munitions. Weapons and ammunition, like bombs, gunpowder, and bullets.

murky. Dark, cloudy, or difficult to see.

oral history. A recorded firsthand account of a historical event.

Pacific Fleet. All of the ships and planes stationed in the Pacific Ocean during World War II.

polyp. A small water animal without a backbone that has a soft body and a mouth surrounded by tentacles.

porthole. A small window in the side of a ship or plane.

ROV. Remotely operated vehicle. Small submarine robots that can be controlled from the surface.

salvage. Removing parts from something broken to use them elsewhere. Relating to Pearl Harbor, it was the act of recovering ships or parts of ships damaged in the Dec. 7th attack to repair and put back into service.

sediment. Particles of rock or sand that settle on the bottom of the seafloor.

solemn. A serious occasion or mood.

stern. The back part of a boat or ship.

superstructure. The part of a ship above the main deck.

turret. A low, steel platform on a tank, plane, or ship, where large guns are mounted. They can be rotated to aim the guns.

veteran. A person who served in the military during a war.

visibility. The distance you can see.

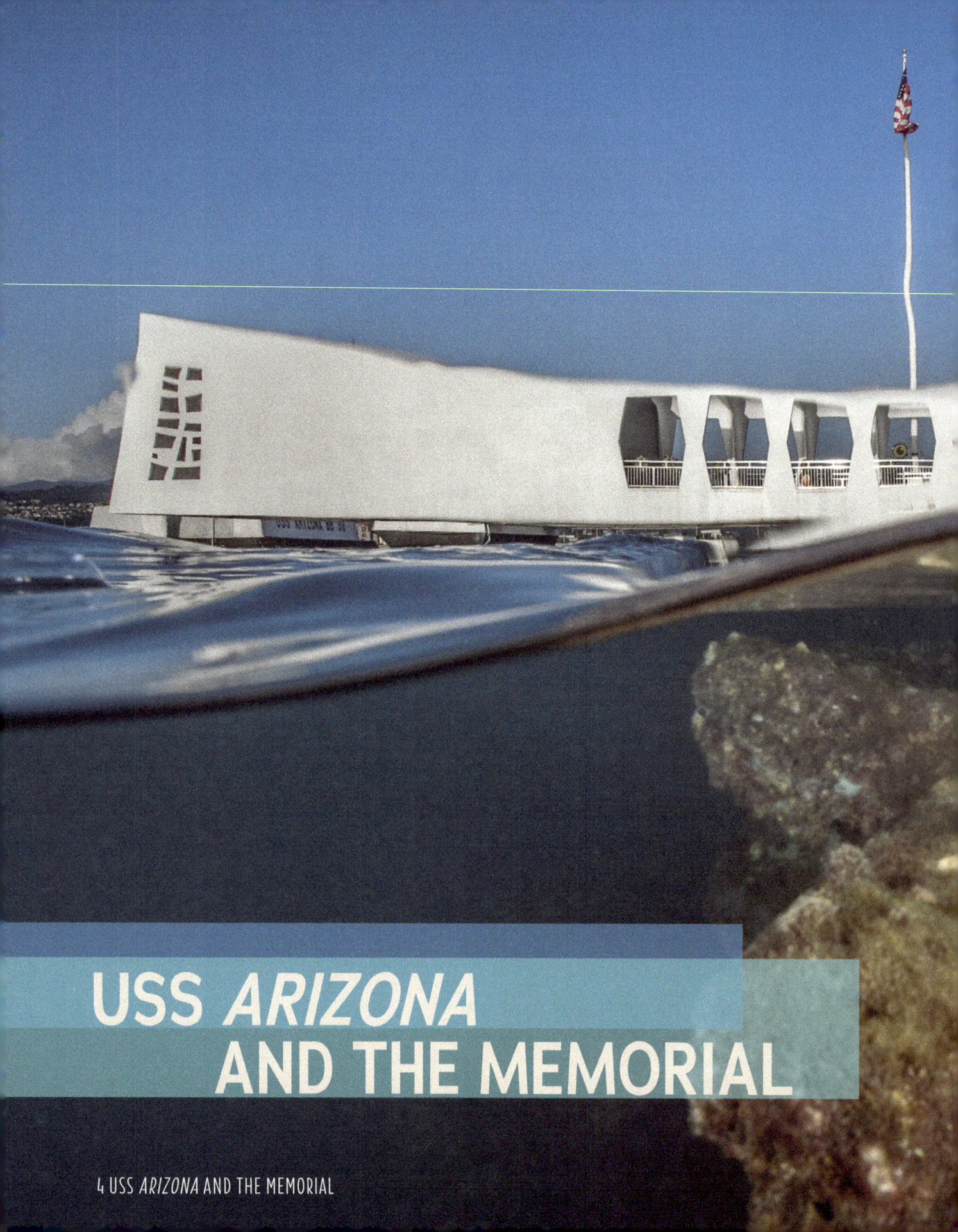

USS *ARIZONA*
AND THE MEMORIAL

The USS *Arizona* Memorial in Pearl Harbor, Hawaii.

HOW DID THE USS *ARIZONA* END UP IN PEARL HARBOR?

The USS *Arizona* is over one hundred years old and was built in the Brooklyn Navy Yard in New York. **Commissioned** into the U.S. Navy in October, 1916, the USS *Arizona* had an adventurous career. She served in World War I, trained in Cuba, visited Turkey, sailed through the Panama Canal, was **modernized** in Norfolk, Virginia, and became a movie star in the film *Here Comes the Navy*. While in Hawaii for training in 1940, the USS *Arizona*, along with the rest of the **Pacific Fleet**, was assigned to stay in Hawaiian waters to discourage the advancing Japanese fleet, since tensions were rising in the Pacific at the beginning of World War II.

During the Japanese attack on Pearl Harbor on December 7, 1941, the USS *Arizona* suffered major damage from bombs dropped by fighter planes. 1,177 U.S. Navy sailors and marines lost their lives on board during the attack, and the ship was sunk. While many attempts were made to save her, she was one of the few ships unable to be **salvaged** after the attack.

DID YOU KNOW?

Ship names are always written in *italics*. There are many prefixes for ship names, which show the ship's duty. This part of the ship's name is not italicized. Some of these prefixes are: USS (United States ship, for active duty navy ships), FV (fishing vessel), RV (research vessel), and SV (sailing vessel). Regardless of their names, ships and submarines are always referred to as female. For example: The USS *Arizona* had 4 sets of 14-inch guns on her deck.

In this photo of the USS *Arizona* Memorial taken from a helicopter, you can see the sunken battleship underwater in Pearl Harbor. The blue sheen drifting from the ship is leaking oil.

THE MEMORIAL

The USS *Arizona* Memorial was dedicated on Memorial Day, May 30, 1962, to remember those who died on December 7, 1941. The Memorial was designed by local Hawaiian architect Alfred Preis, who won a contest with his plan for the white, curved structure. Design rules set by the U.S. Navy stated the Memorial should not touch the ship, and it should span the ship as if it were a bridge. Preis' design followed this rule, and even though it looks like it is resting on top of the ship, the Memorial does not touch the ship at all.

Toward the back of the Memorial, there is the viewing well where visitors can look down into the water and see a portion of the ship. At the far end is the Shrine Room, the most **solemn** place of the Memorial. In it, there is a large, white marble wall with the names of all 1,177 men who gave their lives on December 7, 1941, with the inscription, "TO THE MEMORY OF THE GALLANT MEN HERE ENTOMBED AND THEIR SHIPMATES WHO GAVE THEIR LIVES IN ACTION ON DECEMBER 7, 1941 ON THE U.S.S. ARIZONA." Just in front of the Shrine Room wall on the left and right, there are small marble panels where you can also see the names of the USS *Arizona* survivors chosen to be **interred** with their shipmates once they have passed away. You can learn more about this on page 27. As of January 2018, there were only 5 surviving men left.

OTHER MEMORIALS IN PEARL HARBOR

More than 180 ships and vessels were in Pearl Harbor when the attack began on December 7, 1941. Twenty-one ships were sunk, severely damaged, or required major repairs. The USS *Arizona* and the USS *Utah* still remain in Pearl Harbor.

WHAT IS THE NATIONAL PARK SERVICE?

The National Park Service (also called NPS) is a federal agency that protects and preserves important natural and cultural areas in the United States and its territories for the enjoyment, education, and inspiration of future generations. It currently manages the USS *Arizona* shipwreck and its Memorial, as a part of World War II Valor in the Pacific National Monument, because these sites have historical importance to the American story of World War II. Can you think of any other war memorials that are national park sites?

An NPS flat hat and Hawaiian flower lei in front of the USS *Arizona* Memorial.

An NPS Honor Guard in front of the Shrine Room wall at the USS *Arizona* Memorial.

One of the NPS divers jumping into the water for a dive on the USS *Arizona*.

DIVING ON
THE USS *ARIZONA*

WHY DIVE ON THE USS *ARIZONA*?

Even though the ship's deck is only a few feet underwater and the harbor is only 34 feet deep, it is hard to see the ship without being in the water yourself. Pearl Harbor is **murky** because of its muddy bottom, and strong **currents** stir up the water and keep it cloudy. If managers at the park want to know about the USS *Arizona*, they have to get in and look with their own eyes. Data collected while diving show how the ship is changing by being underwater for many years and what kind of animals live on the ship. Divers also remove objects dropped on the wreck by visitors to the Memorial and place the remains of USS *Arizona* survivors in the wreck for burial. You can learn more about this on page 27.

The No. 1 gun turrett of the USS *Arizona*. It was thought that the No. 1 guns were salvaged immediatly after the Pearl Harbor attack, but they were discovered by NPS divers on their first dive on the ship in 1983.

An NPS diver mapping the galley (kitchen) area of the USS *Arizona*.

A SHORT HISTORY OF DIVING ON THE USS *ARIZONA*

Right after the Pearl Harbor attack, divers from the navy recovered what they could from the wreckage of the USS *Arizona*. The Memorial was built 20 years later in 1962 directly over the wreck. However, divers weren't needed during construction because the support pillars were sunk into the harbor's muddy bottom outside the edges of the ship. Neither the Memorial nor its supporting structures touch the shipwreck below.

The responsibility for the USS *Arizona* and the Memorial was transferred to the National Park Service (NPS) in 1980. Soon after, a specialized team of underwater **archaeologists** from the NPS dived on the wreck and created high-quality maps of the ship. This team developed a new method of underwater mapping that allowed them to make accurate maps despite the shallow, murky water.

Over the next 35 years, resource managers used diving to help them keep a close eye on the ship. They do about 50 dives per year on the site for scientific surveys, photographing the ship, picking up dropped items, and survivor interments.

DIVING IN BLUE JEANS?

In this photo from the 1980s, the diver is wearing blue jeans. The thick fabric will not tear and will protect the divers from the sharp metal on the ship. Today's wetsuits are easy to take on and off, but in the 1980s people who did lots of dives in warm water often wore jeans or canvas jumpsuits instead of the thick, stiff, rubber wetsuits available at the time.

An NPS archaeologist at a **porthole** in the stern of the ship during mapping dives in 1986.

Diving for fun (called recreational diving) is not allowed on the USS *Arizona*. Unlike many other shipwrecks popular for scuba diving, the USS *Arizona* lies in an active duty U.S. Navy base, and security must be maintained. The ship is also a war grave, so the site is closed to recreational diving out of respect for the lives lost on board. The NPS strives to bring visitors below the surface and closer to the ship by hosting live broadcasts by NPS divers underwater. Recordings of these "live dives" can be found on the park's website, www.nps.gov/valr.

NPS DIVE TEAM

Who dives on the USS *Arizona*? The team of divers who regularly dive on the ship work for the National Park Service. They are archaeologists, biologists, photographers, law enforcement rangers, and other resource managers.

An NPS diver shines a light into a sediment-filled hatch that leads to the crew's sleeping area.

The Memorial from a diver's point of view.

The NPS archaeologists rediscovered the No. 1 guns on their first dive on the USS *Arizona* in 1983.

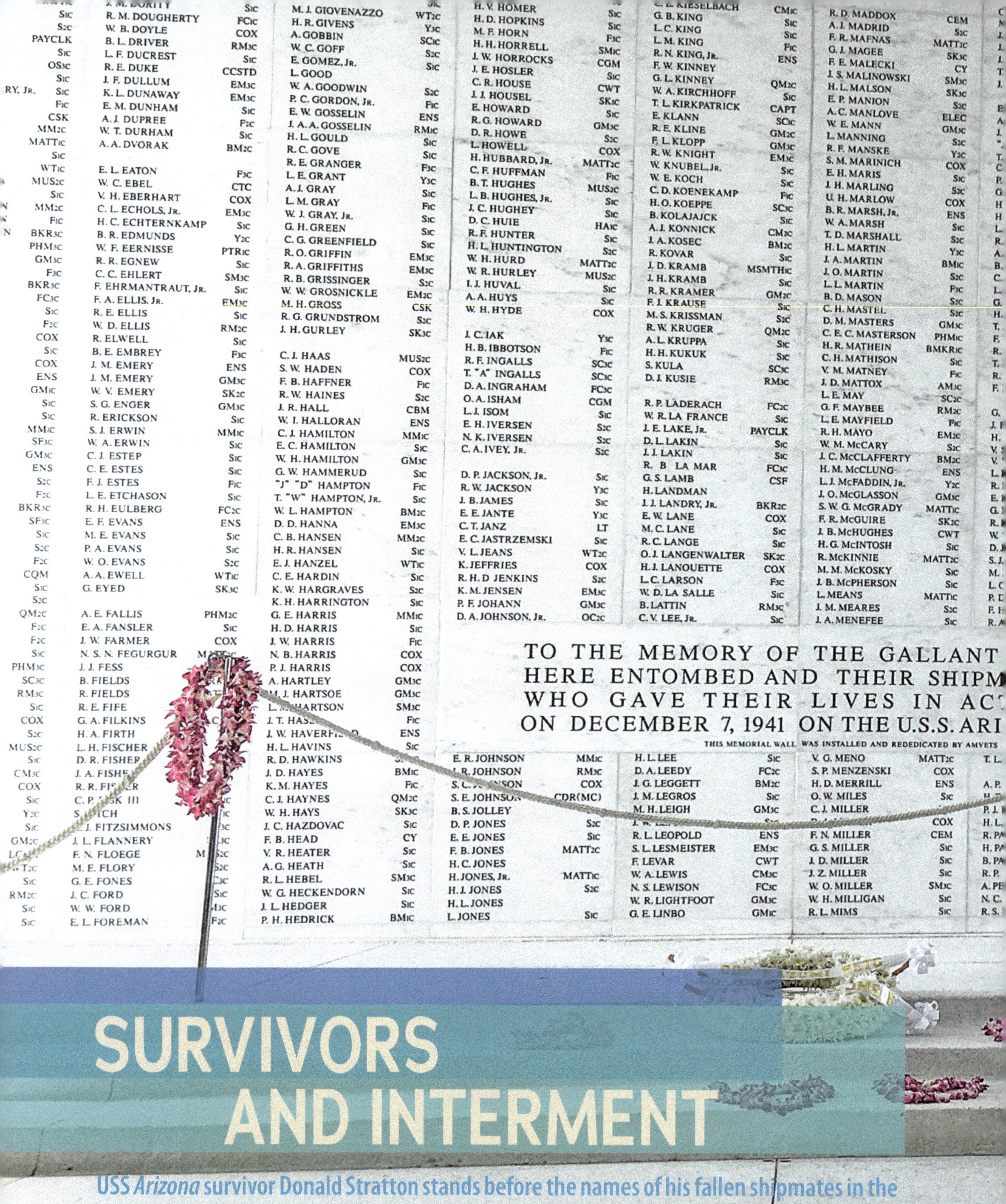

Orphan ratings (leftmost, names cropped):
SIC · PAYCLK · SIC · OSIC · SIC · RY, JR. SIC · FIC · CSK · MM2C · MATT1C · SIC · WT1C · MUS2C · SIC · MM2C · FIC · BKR3C · PHM1C · GM3C · F3C · BKR3C · FC2C · SIC · SIC · COX · SIC · COX · ENS · GM1C · SIC · SIC · MM2C · SF3C · GM3C · ENS · S2C · F2C · BKR3C · SF3C · SIC · S2C · F2C · CQM · SIC · S2C · QM2C · FIC · F2C · SIC · PHM3C · SC3C · RM1C · SIC · COX · S2C · MUS2C · SIC · CM3C · COX · SIC · Y3C · SIC · GM2C · LCDR · WT1C · SIC · RM2C · SIC

Name	Rate
R. M. DOUGHERTY	FC1C
W. B. DOYLE	COX
B. L. DRIVER	RM1C
L. F. DUCREST	SIC
R. E. DUKE	CCSTD
J. F. DULLUM	EM3C
K. L. DUNAWAY	EM3C
E. M. DUNHAM	SIC
A. J. DUPREE	F2C
W. T. DURHAM	SIC
A. A. DVORAK	BM2C
E. L. EATON	F3C
W. C. EBEL	CTC
V. H. EBERHART	COX
C. L. ECHOLS, JR.	EM3C
H. C. ECHTERNKAMP	SIC
B. R. EDMUNDS	Y2C
W. F. EERNISSE	PTR1C
R. R. EGNEW	SIC
C. C. EHLERT	SM3C
F. EHRMANTRAUT, JR.	SIC
F. A. ELLIS, JR.	EM3C
R. E. ELLIS	SIC
W. D. ELLIS	RM2C
R. ELWELL	SIC
B. E. EMERY	F3C
J. M. EMERY	ENS
J. M. EMERY	GM3C
W. V. EMERY	SK2C
S. G. ENGER	GM3C
R. ERICKSON	SIC
S. J. ERWIN	MM1C
W. A. ERWIN	SIC
C. J. ESTEP	SIC
C. E. ESTES	SIC
F. J. ESTES	FIC
L. E. ETCHASON	SIC
R. H. EULBERG	FC2C
E. F. EVANS	ENS
M. E. EVANS	SIC
P. A. EVANS	SIC
W. O. EVANS	S2C
A. A. EWELL	WT1C
G. EYED	SK3C
A. E. FALLIS	PHM2C
E. A. FANSLER	
J. W. FARMER	COX
N. S. N. FEGURGUR	MATT1C
J. J. FESS	
B. FIELDS	
R. FIELDS	
R. E. FIFE	
G. A. FILKINS	
H. A. FIRTH	
L. H. FISCHER	
D. R. FISHER	
J. A. FISHER	
R. R. FISHER	
C. P. FISK III	
S. FITCH	
J. J. FITZSIMMONS	
J. L. FLANNERY	
F. N. FLOEGE	M
M. E. FLORY	S2C
G. E. FONES	
J. C. FORD	
W. W. FORD	M1C
E. L. FOREMAN	F2C

Name	Rate
M. J. GIOVENAZZO	WT2C
H. R. GIVENS	Y3C
A. GOBBIN	SC1C
W. C. GOFF	S2C
E. GOMEZ, JR.	SIC
L. GOOD	SIC
W. A. GOODWIN	SIC
P. C. GORDON, JR.	S2C
E. W. GOSSELIN	ENS
J. A. A. GOSSELIN	RM1C
H. L. GOULD	SIC
R. C. GOVE	SIC
R. E. GRANGER	F3C
L. E. GRANT	Y3C
A. J. GRAY	SIC
L. M. GRAY	F1C
W. J. GRAY, JR.	SIC
G. H. GREEN	SIC
C. G. GREENFIELD	SIC
R. O. GRIFFIN	EM3C
R. A. GRIFFITHS	EM3C
R. B. GRISSINGER	S2C
W. W. GROSNICKLE	EM2C
M. H. GROSS	CSK
R. G. GRUNDSTROM	SIC
J. H. GURLEY	SK3C
C. J. HAAS	MUS2C
S. W. HADEN	COX
F. B. HAFFNER	FIC
R. W. HAINES	S2C
J. R. HALL	CBM
W. I. HALLORAN	ENS
C. J. HAMILTON	MM1C
E. C. HAMILTON	SIC
W. H. HAMILTON	GM3C
G. W. HAMMERUD	SIC
"J" "D" HAMPTON	FIC
T. "W" HAMPTON, JR.	SIC
W. L. HAMPTON	BM2C
D. D. HANNA	EM3C
C. B. HANSEN	MM2C
H. R. HANSEN	SIC
E. J. HANZEL	WT1C
C. E. HARDIN	SIC
K. W. HARGRAVES	S2C
K. H. HARRINGTON	SIC
G. E. HARRIS	MM1C
H. D. HARRIS	SIC
J. W. HARRIS	FIC
N. B. HARRIS	COX
P. J. HARRIS	COX
A. HARTLEY	GM3C
M. J. HARTSOE	GM3C
L. M. HARTSON	SM3C
J. T. HASL...	FIC
J. W. HAVERFIELD	ENS
H. L. HAVINS	SIC
R. D. HAWKINS	
J. D. HAYES	BM1C
K. M. HAYES	FIC
C. J. HAYNES	QM2C
W. H. HAYS	SK3C
J. C. HAZDOVAC	SIC
F. B. HEAD	CY
V. R. HEATER	SIC
A. G. HEATH	SIC
R. L. HEBEL	SM3C
W. G. HECKENDORN	SIC
J. L. HEDGER	SIC
P. H. HEDRICK	BM1C

Name	Rate
H. V. HOMER	SIC
H. D. HOPKINS	SIC
M. F. HORN	SIC
H. H. HORRELL	F1C
J. W. HORROCKS	SM1C
J. E. HOSLER	SIC
C. R. HOUSE	CWT
J. J. HOUSEL	SK1C
E. HOWARD	SIC
R. G. HOWARD	GM3C
D. R. HOWE	S2C
L. HOWELL	COX
H. HUBBARD, JR.	MATT2C
C. F. HUFFMAN	FIC
B. T. HUGHES	MUS2C
L. B. HUGHES, JR.	SIC
J. C. HUGHEY	SIC
D. C. HUIE	HA1C
R. F. HUNTER	SIC
H. L. HUNTINGTON	SIC
W. H. HURD	MATT2C
W. R. HURLEY	MUS2C
I. J. HUVAL	SIC
A. A. HUYS	SIC
W. H. HYDE	COX
J. C. IAK	Y3C
H. B. IBBOTSON	FIC
R. F. INGALLS	SC3C
T. "A" INGALLS	SC3C
D. A. INGRAHAM	FC3C
O. A. ISHAM	CGM
L. J. ISOM	SIC
E. H. IVERSEN	SIC
N. K. IVERSEN	S2C
C. A. IVEY, JR.	S2C
D. P. JACKSON, JR.	SIC
R. W. JACKSON	Y3C
J. B. JAMES	SIC
E. E. JANTE	Y3C
C. T. JANZ	LT
E. C. JASTRZEMSKI	SIC
V. L. JEANS	WT2C
K. JEFFRIES	COX
R. H. D JENKINS	S2C
K. M. JENSEN	EM3C
P. F. JOHANN	GM3C
D. A. JOHNSON, JR.	OC2C
E. R. JOHNSON	MM1C
R. JOHNSON	RM1C
S. C. JOHNSON	COX
S. E. JOHNSON	CDR(MC)
B. S. JOLLEY	SIC
D. P. JONES	S2C
E. E. JONES	SIC
F. B. JONES	MATT2C
H. C. JONES	SIC
H. JONES, JR.	MATT1C
H. J. JONES	S2C
H. L. JONES	SIC
L. JONES	SIC

Name	Rate
G. B. KING	SIC
L. C. KING	SIC
L. M. KING	SIC
R. N. KING, JR.	F1C
F. W. KINNEY	ENS
G. L. KINNEY	SIC
W. A. KIRCHHOFF	SIC
T. L. KIRKPATRICK	CAPT
E. KLANN	SC1C
R. E. KLINE	SIC
F. L. KLOPP	GM2C
R. W. KNIGHT	EM3C
W. KNUBEL, JR.	SIC
W. E. KOCH	SIC
C. D. KOENEKAMP	FIC
H. O. KOEPPE	SC3C
B. KOLAJAJCK	SIC
A. J. KONNICK	CM2C
J. A. KOSEC	BM2C
R. KOVAR	SIC
J. D. KRAMB	MSMTH1C
J. H. KRAMB	SIC
R. R. KRAMER	GM2C
F. J. KRAUSE	SIC
M. S. KRISSMAN	S2C
R. W. KRUGER	QM2C
A. L. KRUPPA	SIC
H. H. KUKUK	SIC
S. KULA	SC3C
D. J. KUSIE	RM3C
R. P. LADERACH	FC2C
W. R. LA FRANCE	SIC
J. E. LAKE, JR.	PAYCLK
D. L. LAKIN	SIC
J. J. LAKIN	SIC
R. B LA MAR	SIC
G. S. LAMB	CSF
H. LANDMAN	SIC
J. J. LANDRY, JR.	BKR2C
E. W. LANE	COX
M. C. LANE	SIC
R. C. LANGE	SIC
O. J. LANGENWALTER	SK2C
H. J. LANOUETTE	COX
L. C. LARSON	FIC
W. D. LA SALLE	RM2C
B. LATTIN	SIC
C. V. LEE, JR.	SIC
H. L. LEE	SIC
D. A. LEEDY	FC2C
J. G. LEGGETT	BM2C
J. M. LEGROS	SIC
M. H. LEIGH	GM3C
R. L. LEOPOLD	ENS
S. L. LESMEISTER	EM3C
F. LEVAR	CWT
W. A. LEWIS	CM3C
N. S. LEWISON	FC3C
W. R. LIGHTFOOT	GM3C
G. E. LINBO	GM3C

Name	Rate
R. D. MADDOX	CEM
A. J. MADRID	SIC
F. R. MAFNAS	MATT1C
G. J. MAGEE	SK3C
F. E. MALECKI	CY
J. S. MALINOWSKI	SM3C
H. L. MALSON	SK3C
E. P. MANION	SIC
A. C. MANLOVE	ELEC
W. E. MANN	GM3C
L. MANNING	S2C
R. F. MANSKE	Y3C
S. M. MARINICH	COX
E. H. MARIS	SIC
J. H. MARLING	SIC
U. H. MARLOW	COX
B. R. MARSH, JR.	ENS
W. A. MARSH	SIC
T. D. MARSHALL	S2C
H. L. MARTIN	Y3C
J. A. MARTIN	BM1C
J. O. MARTIN	SIC
L. L. MARTIN	F3C
B. D. MASON	SIC
C. H. MASTEL	SIC
D. M. MASTERS	GM3C
C. E. C. MASTERSON	PHM1C
H. R. MATHEIN	BMKR1C
C. H. MATHISON	SIC
V. M. MATNEY	FIC
J. D. MATTOX	AM3C
L. E. MAY	SC2C
G. F. MAYBEE	RM2C
L. E. MAYFIELD	FIC
R. H. MAYO	EM2C
W. M. McCARY	S2C
J. C. McCLAFFERTY	BM2C
H. M. McCLUNG	ENS
L. J. McFADDIN	Y2C
J. O. McGLASSON	GM3C
S. W. G. McGRADY	MATT1C
F. R. McGUIRE	SK2C
J. B. McHUGHES	CWT
H. G. McINTOSH	SIC
R. McKINNIE	MATT2C
M. M. McKOSKY	SIC
J. B. McPHERSON	SIC
L. MEANS	MATT1C
J. M. MEARES	SIC
J. A. MENEFEE	SIC

Name	Rate
V. G. MENO	MATT2C
S. P. MENZENSKI	COX
H. D. MERRILL	ENS
O. W. MILES	SIC
C. J. MILLER	SIC
	COX
F. N. MILLER	CEM
G. S. MILLER	SIC
J. D. MILLER	SIC
J. Z. MILLER	SIC
W. O. MILLER	SM3C
W. H. MILLIGAN	SIC
R. L. MIMS	SIC

Memorial inscription (center):

TO THE MEMORY OF THE GALLANT
HERE ENTOMBED AND THEIR SHIPM[ATES]
WHO GAVE THEIR LIVES IN ACT[ION]
ON DECEMBER 7, 1941 ON THE U.S.S. ARI[ZONA]

THIS MEMORIAL WALL WAS INSTALLED AND REDEDICATED BY AMVETS

SURVIVORS AND INTERMENT

USS *Arizona* survivor Donald Stratton stands before the names of his fallen shipmates in the Memorial Shrine Room in August 2016.

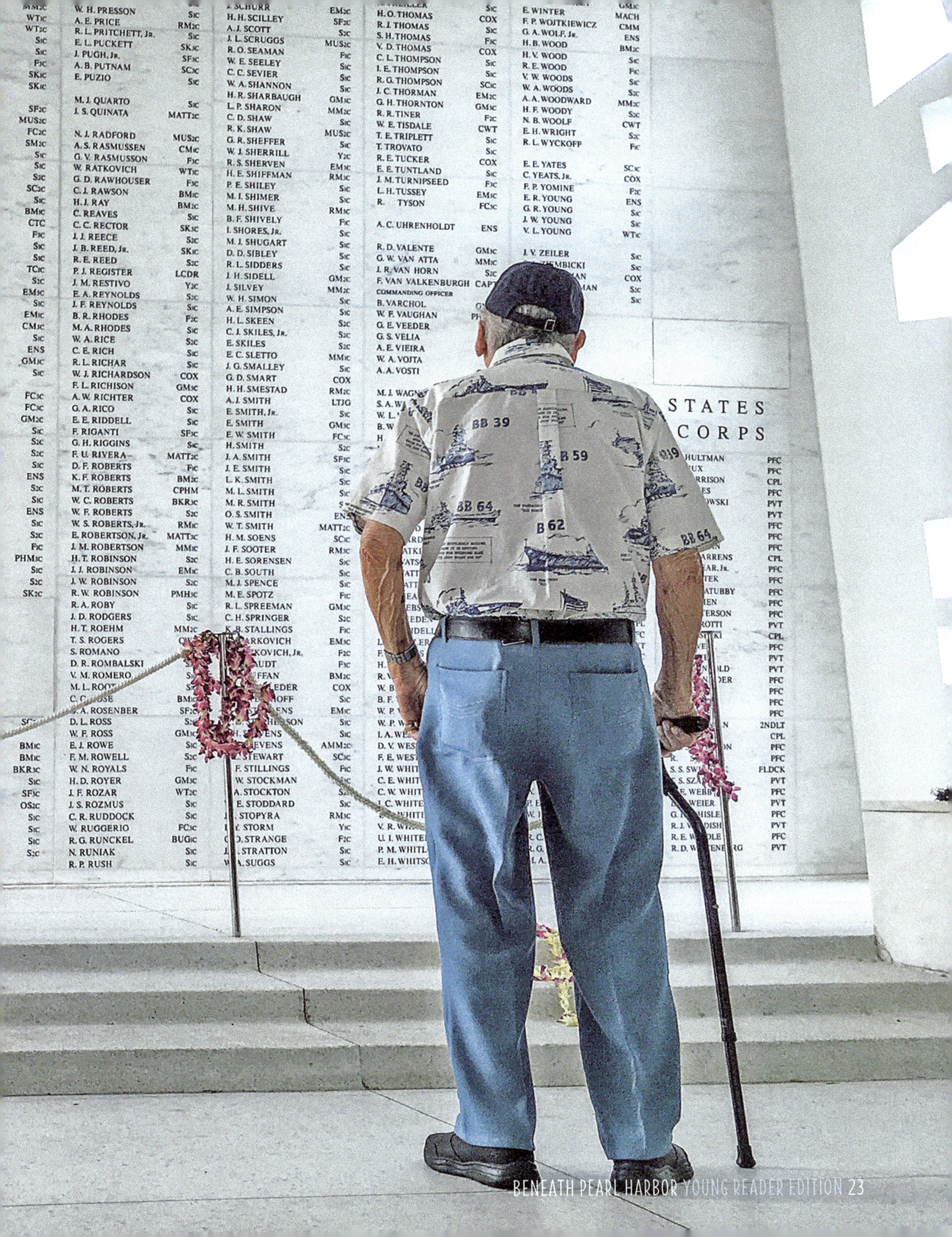
STATES
CORPS
BB 39
B 59
BB 64
B 62
BB 64

SURVIVORS

Out of the USS *Arizona*'s crew of 1,511 sailors and marines, only 334 men survived. Most of them were injured in the attack, but they worked bravely and tirelessly to help their fellow crewmates as the bombs fell. Although the losses on the USS *Arizona* were the most numerous, there were also many other casualties in and around Pearl Harbor on December 7, 1941. There are countless stories of selflessness and heroism from that day, which is why victims and survivors of the attack are treated with such respect and reverence.

Members of the military during WWII are part of the "Greatest Generation," the generation of people who grew up during the **Great Depression** and had to overcome many obstacles to experience the American Dream. They lived during a time when food, jobs, and luxuries were scarce, and they had to work hard to support their families. They brought their strong work ethic, humility, dedication, and sense of personal responsibility with them into the military. Because of these traits, many survivors went on to have long military careers even though they were hurt during the attack on Pearl Harbor.

Most of the survivors have passed away. Their stories have passed with them, but many of the survivors have recorded **oral histories** with the NPS about their experience during the attack. These are **archived** and available to the public.

USS *Arizona* survivors Lauren Bruner, John Anderson, Lou Conter, and Donald Stratton at a ceremony on the USS *Arizona* Memorial in 2014.

Captain Charles Freeman escorts President Herbert Hoover during crew inspection on USS *Arizona*'s main deck, March 21, 1931.

INTERMENT ON THE USS *ARIZONA*

WHAT IS INTERMENT?

Interment is another word for burial. When the USS *Arizona* survivors have their remains placed in the wreck, it is referred to as interment.

The USS *Arizona* survivors are given a special option for burial. Normally, U.S. military members have the right to be buried in a U.S. military cemetery with an **honor guard**. For survivors of the USS *Arizona*, they can choose to have their cremated remains interred underwater within the ship, along with a military funeral service on the Memorial in Pearl Harbor. Generally this happens on Dec. 7th of the year the survivor has passed away. Survivors choose to be buried this way so that they may be laid to rest with their fellow shipmates.

When survivors are interred, a special team of divers from NPS and the U.S. Navy take the urn holding the cremated remains from the family after the funeral service and swim to the open **barbette** of the fourth gun **turret**. At the floor of the barbette, there is a passageway that opens to the inside of the ship. The urn is placed inside this passageway and the survivor rejoins his crewmates aboard the USS *Arizona*. The ceremony and interment are solemn occasions, but they both honor and fulfill the final wishes of the survivors.

Interment of USS *Arizona* survivor Ensign Joseph K. Langdell on December 7, 2015. His sons pass an urn to an NPS diver for burial inside the USS *Arizona* (right). An NPS diver places the urn inside the No. 4 Barbette (left).

LEAKING OIL

A diver surfaces from a dive on the USS *Arizona* during a storm, where leaking oil has concentrated on the water surface.

WHY IS THERE OIL LEAKING FROM THE SHIP?

The ship was filled with fuel just before the attack. When full, she carried nearly 1.5 million gallons of **Bunker-C oil**. Like all fuel, this oil is flammable, and after the attack the ship burned for 2.5 days. It is **estimated** that about one-third of the oil (500,000 gallons) remains on board.

The oil bunkers (tanks) that held the fuel were damaged during the attack, causing many of them to leak, even today. The oil that leaks out of the bunkers and up through the ship can be seen from the Memorial as a rainbow-colored sheen on the water's surface. According to studies by the NPS, the ship still leaks 2-9 quarts of oil each day.

WHY DOES OIL FLOAT?

Oil is less dense than water, and it will always rise to the water's surface. You can see this for yourself by putting a few drops of cooking oil into a glass of water.

WHY CAN'T THE OIL BE REMOVED?

Many ships have a single fuel tank, but battleships have hundreds of tanks to prevent huge fuel losses if struck by an enemy torpedo. The USS *Arizona* has over 200 fuel tanks, many of which are in the deepest part of the ship now sunk in the mud of Pearl Harbor. Trying to remove the oil from the ship would destroy the **hull** and disturb the final resting place of nearly 1,000 men. NPS scientists regularly study the ship's hull to measure how it changes over time. It is estimated that it will last more than 150 years before it collapses. There is a current emergency plan for an unexpected oil spill, just in case.

Underwater, oil floats up from the ship in individual droplets. Once the droplets reach the water's surface, they break apart and the oil spreads out in a rainbow-colored sheen which can be seen from the Memorial.

Oil released from the ship drifts through this underwater view of the Memorial. Although divers are often the subject of many tourist photos, NPS divers try to work in view of 1,300 visitors daily without drawing attention to diving operations.

An NPS diver sets up a camera to capture a 360° photograph of the USS *Arizona*'s **catapult** base.

SEEK AND STUDY

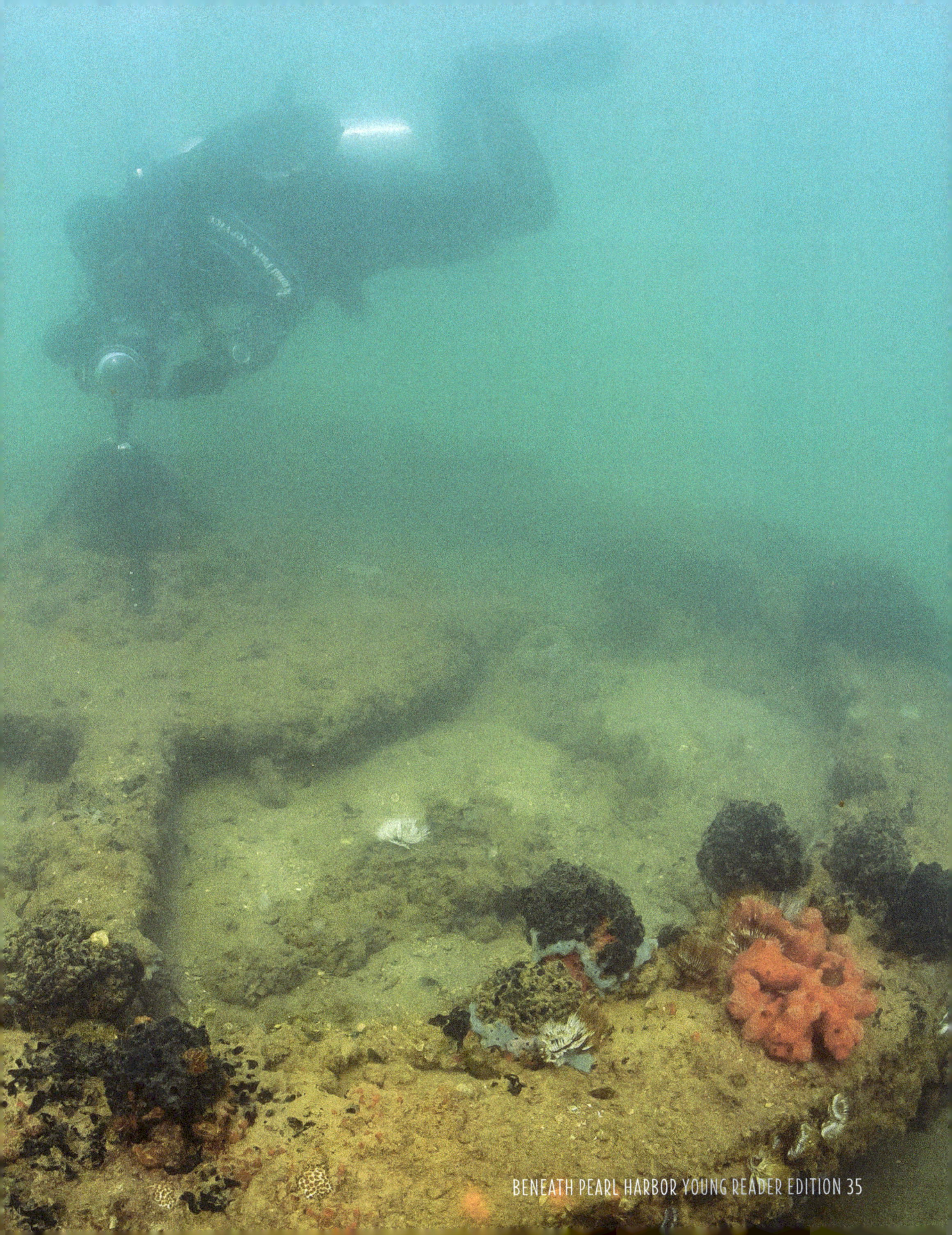

WHY DO WE STUDY THE USS *ARIZONA*?

The wreck of the USS *Arizona* has been underwater for almost 80 years. Over the years, the salt in the seawater causes the ship's metal hull to **corrode**. This could cause the hull to collapse and create an oil spill in Pearl Harbor. NPS managers regularly study the ship and how it is breaking down so they can work to preserve it for future generations and protect the environment.

Diving is a great tool for studying the USS *Arizona*. Divers collect samples of the ship's metal structures and the leaking oil. They also set up scientific equipment on the ship to collect data about water quality and the ship's small movements as it shifts in the harbor's muddy bottom over time. The USS *Arizona* is much easier to study than shipwrecks in deeper, colder, and more remote waters like in the open ocean or the Great Lakes. It lies in a body of water next to a major city so it's easy to get to, it is shallow, and the water is warm. Keeping track of how the USS *Arizona* **deteriorates** helps scientists understand how other shipwrecks are aging as well. Scientists can also test out new scientific methods at the USS *Arizona* before using them at other underwater World War II sites.

An NPS diver gives the "OK" signal while setting up a piece of scientific equipment on the ship (left).

An NPS diver experiments with a tool to measure the ship's hull thickness (right).

WHAT KINDS OF RESEARCH HAPPEN ON THE SHIP?

Photography and 3D imaging: Helps track changes over time in the visible features of the ship and the artifacts on the deck. Photography has an important role for the shipwreck. While maps can show how the wreck lies on the seafloor, photographs allow us to see through the eyes of the diver.

Oil Collection: NPS wants to know how much oil is being released from the ship. If that amount changes, it could mean that there is a new leak inside the ship. They measure this by placing a small tent over locations where oil is leaking and measuring how much oil they collect over a specific period of time.

Coupon Sampling: Scientists collect small samples of the ship's metal hull to measure how it is weakening over time. They have learned that different parts of the ship weaken at different rates. This helps them estimate how long it will be before an oil spill or big change in the ship's structure.

Superpoints: This method measures tiny movements of the ship over time. By measuring known points on the ship over the years and seeing how they shift using advanced GPS units, scientists can tell if the ship is sinking deeper into the mud or tilting to one side. The movements are so small they can't be seen by our eyes but can be recorded with precise measurements.

Mapping: Whether it's of an ancient Roman city or an underwater shipwreck, making maps is an important part of archaeology. There are many ways to make maps. The NPS divers who first mapped the wreck of the USS *Arizona* used a new method involving string and angles to help them map the ship in the murky water of Pearl Harbor. In more recent years, scientists have been experimenting with new technology like laser scanning to make digital maps.

DID YOU KNOW?

The **visibility** in Pearl Harbor is only about 6 feet. That means divers can only see 6 feet in any direction. Imagine trying to draw a map of a 600-foot-long ship when you can only see 6 feet in front of you!

Following pages: On the left is a draft of the first map made of the wreck by divers in the early 1980s. The map on the right was made in 2015 using 3D sonar technology. How are they different?

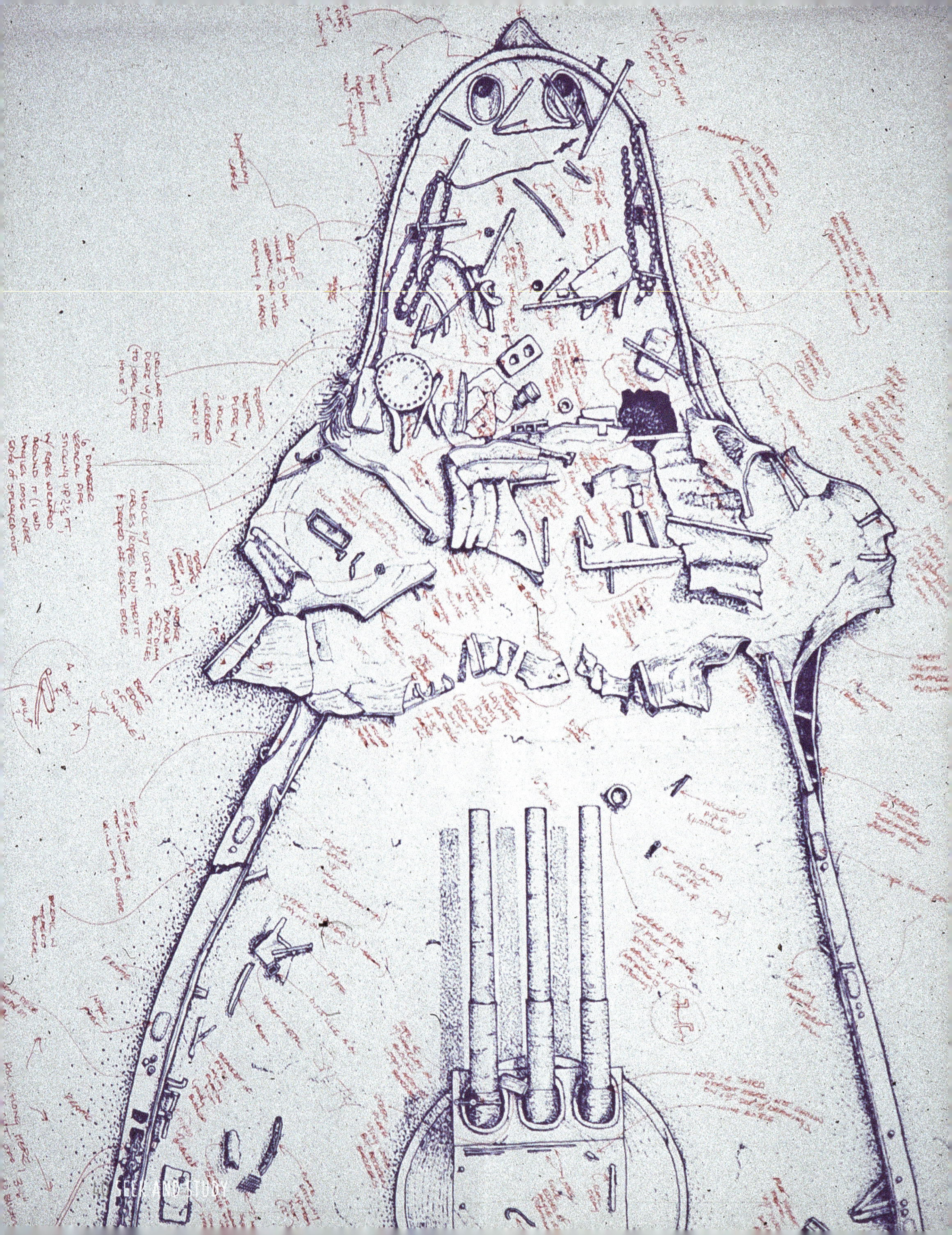

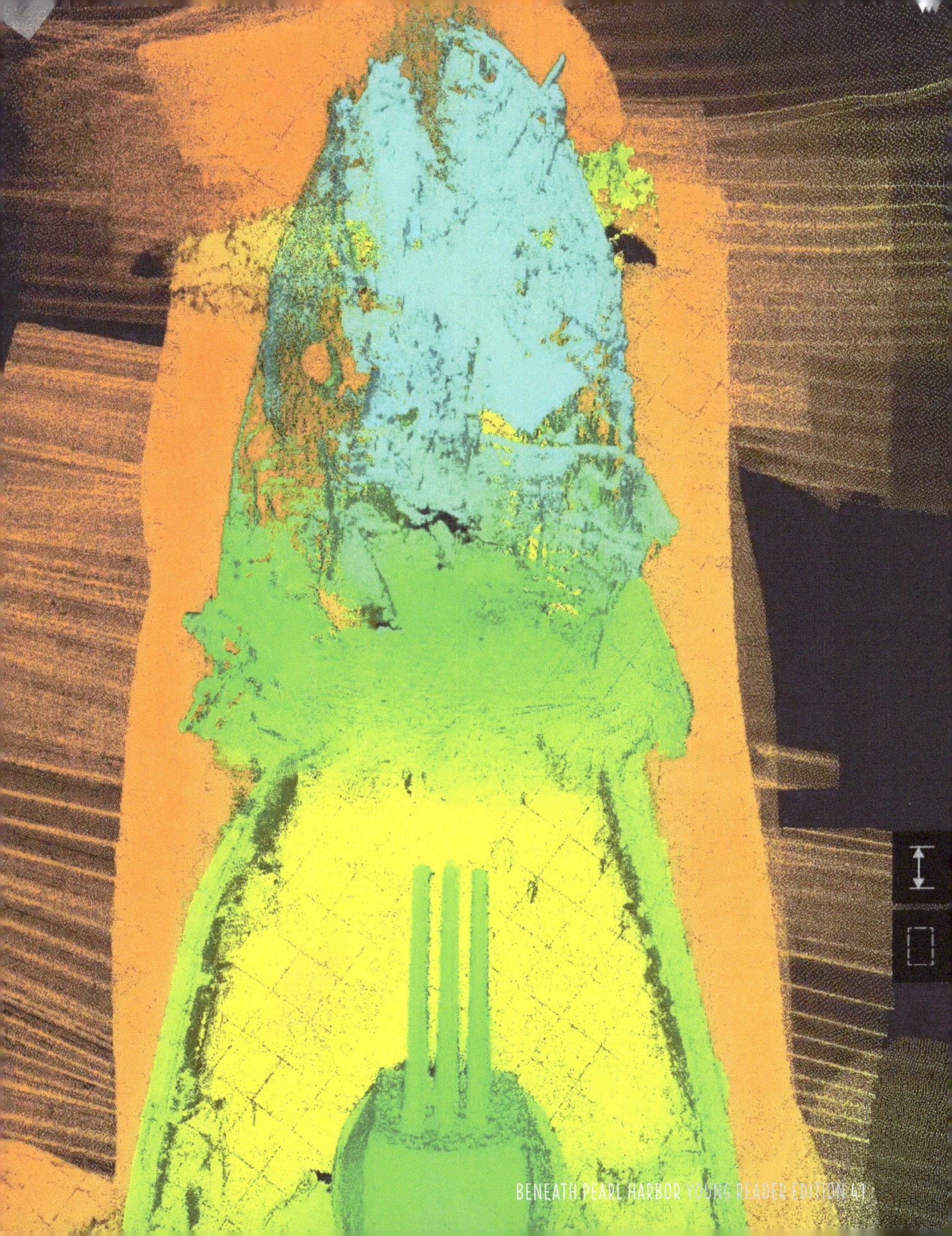

BRINGING ARTIFACTS TO THE SURFACE WITH NEW TECHNOLOGY

One of the most well-known artifacts found on the deck of the USS *Arizona* was the Coke bottle. In the 1940s during the Great Depression, as you read on page 24, men and women worked anywhere they could. Many joined the U.S. Navy and were sent thousands of miles away from home without cell phones, texting, or video chatting to keep in touch with family and friends. Often they found themselves homesick. Finding items reminding these brave men and women of home became important. Coca-Cola was something found in Hawaii and tasted exactly the same as it did back home.

When NPS divers discovered this Coke bottle on the deck of the ship, they first thought it was trash. Upon closer inspection, they saw it was a historic bottle and it was located in the area of the USS *Arizona*'s ice cream shop (called a gedunk). This bottle was most likely on the ship December 7, 1941.

NPS is using new technology to bring the ship and its history to the surface. One way is by using 3D printing to re-create artifacts on the ship, so they can be seen on the surface by visitors. Here you can see the Coke bottle as it currently lies on the ship (top) and the 3D printed version (bottom). You can learn more about the USS *Arizona*'s artifacts on page 54.

WHAT ABOUT YOU?

Have you ever gone away to summer camp? Gone on a trip away from home with or without your family? What would you want to bring along so you wouldn't feel homesick?

INSIDE THE SHIP

This view of the Division Marine Office in the stern of the ship shows a nearly buried writing desk. By shining high-powered lights through the few open portholes, photographers can take photos of cabins on the second deck.

HOW AND WHY DOES NPS EXPLORE INSIDE THE SHIP?

By using remotely operated vehicles called **ROV**s, scientists and managers can explore the inside of the ship. Human divers never go inside, both out of respect for the sailors and marines who lost their lives on board during the Pearl Harbor attack and because it can be dangerous for the divers. ROVs can be controlled from the surface, just like a remote-controlled car or plane. The ROVs sent into the USS *Arizona* have cameras, allowing the operator to see a live video from inside the ship. The ROVs also have lights and special equipment to measure characteristics of the water, including temperature and dissolved oxygen. This helps managers understand the conditions deep inside the ship.

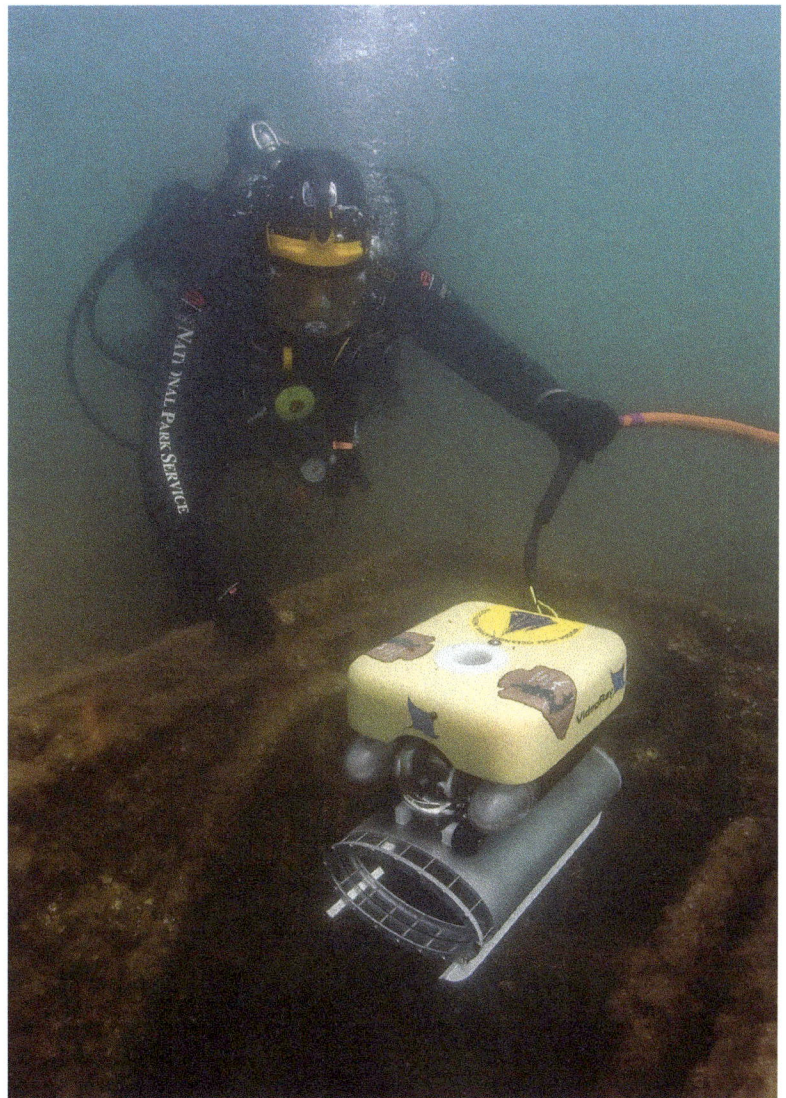

This prototype ROV incorporates a 3D camera to help the operator control it inside the ship. Using 3D cameras also allows scientists to measure distances through the camera (left).

An NPS diver carefully guides an ROV into the ship through an open hatch on the USS *Arizona's* deck (right).

WHAT CAN BE SEEN INSIDE?

It is very dark inside the ship, so nothing can be seen beyond the reach of lights attached to the ROVs or lights that divers shine through the **portholes**. Items on the floor of the rooms and corridors can't be seen because they are covered in several feet of **sediment**. However, light fixtures hanging from the ceiling and furniture (like beds, desks, and tables) can be observed. The walls are covered with **encrusting marine life**.

A conference table and overturned chair with exposed springs located in the sediment-filled admiral's cabin. The light fixture still hangs down from the ceiling.

ARE THERE BODIES?

We know that nearly 1,000 sailors and marines who perished on the USS *Arizona* were never recovered. Their remains have since been either buried by sediment in and around the ship, or they have been decomposed. Divers do not see bodies or body parts on the ship, and the ROVs don't see any inside the ship.

THE JACKET

This uniform jacket hangs in an officer's stateroom on the ship's third deck. It was discovered during an ROV exploration of the USS *Arizona*'s stern in 2016. Using historical maps, researchers determined it belonged to First Lieutenant John Paul Coursey of the U.S. Marine Corps. Lt. Coursey survived the attack and served in many locations in the Pacific throughout World War II.

The excellent condition of this jacket showed the ship's managers that conditions deep inside the ship were cold, low in oxygen, and good for preservation. Scientific tools carried by the ROV gave them more specific details about the water quality this far inside the ship. This is important information for managers to calculate corrosion that will affect the strength of the ship's hull over time.

Lt. Coursey's jacket.

An ROV investigates a sink and vanity in a stateroom on the USS *Arizona*'s second deck.

ARTIFACTS

Tagged artifacts from a sailor's shaving kit.

WHAT IS AN ARTIFACT?

An **artifact** is an object found at the site from the time of the attack rather than a new object like marine litter or coins. Artifacts help paint the picture of what life was like at the time of the attack. It may help to think of the USS *Arizona* wreck as a museum, and the artifacts are the objects inside the museum that tell the story of that time period and the people who lived and worked on the ship.

After a ship in Pearl Harbor nearly collided with the Memorial in 2015, a survey discovered a shoe that had been newly uncovered on the deck.

Bowls from the ship's dining area (above) and rounds of ammunition (below).

WHY AND HOW DOES NPS TRACK ARTIFACTS ON THE SHIP?

As with any **historic site**, artifacts on the ship have been tagged, **inventoried**, and mapped. Some of the well-known artifacts on the USS *Arizona*'s deck include glass bottles, cooking pots and dishes from the galley (ship's kitchen), a sailor's shaving kit, and a fire hose. NPS divers regularly survey the artifacts on the deck to check their locations and condition.

COINS ON THE DECK

Many visitors throw coins onto the wreck from the Memorial, but this practice can be harmful to the ship. As the coins corrode in the saltwater, they can increase corrosion of the ship's metal surfaces as well. As with all National Park sites, it's best to "leave no trace" so that future visitors can enjoy them as much as we do.

A glass bottle with an NPS artifact tag on the deck of the USS *Arizona*.

Corroding coins tossed onto the deck by visitors on the Memorial.

NATURE

Bright sponges and feather worms on the USS *Arizona*'s stern.

A seahorse on the USS *Arizona*.

NATURE TAKES OVER

Over the years, marine life has made its home on board. Most of the ship's deck is encrusted with colorful sea sponges, feather worms, and sea cucumbers. There are also fish, crabs, and sea stars that live on the wreck. Some fish like Hawaiian sergeants, snappers, angelfish, and golden trevallies are often seen by divers. Sometimes, divers get lucky and see rarer creatures, like a seahorse or a pufferfish.

Golden trevallies swim across the USS *Arizona's* **bow.**

Over the past two decades, the USS *Arizona* has become a living reef in the once polluted waters of Pearl Harbor. A variety of life including corals and schooling fish now call the ship home. Here a tiny crab hides among the coral polyps on a reef growing mid-ship on the the USS *Arizona*.

CORALS

As the water quality in Pearl Harbor improves, corals have begun growing on the wreck of the USS *Arizona*. Corals are very small colonial animals. Each individual animal is called a **polyp**, and it builds a limestone **exoskeleton** shared with neighboring polyps to create large, rocky structures called coral reefs. Corals are very sensitive and can become sick or injured from poor water quality, high water temperatures, and touching, which is why they should never be touched underwater. Even though they may look like colorful rocks, they are alive and can be easily damaged.

Recently NPS scientists have been studying how fast these corals grow so they can understand how much extra weight and stress the corals could be putting on the ship's structure. With warming sea-surface temperatures in Hawaii in the past few years, many of the corals on the wreck have been damaged by **coral bleaching**. Time will tell if they will recover.

A dense coral colony grows on what once was a ventilation shaft mid-ship, just below the Memorial.

This long, soft creature is called a sea cucumber. It feeds by filtering algae from the water, sand, and mud.

ARE THERE SHARKS?

Yes there are! But they are very rarely seen by divers on the ship. More often, the divers see sea turtles and eagle rays.

A spotted eagle ray gliding in the waters of Pearl Harbor.

HONORING THE PAST
INSPIRING THE FUTURE

U.S. Navy sailors stand at attention while sailing past the USS *Arizona* Memorial on the 75th Commemoration of the December 7th attack in 2016.

NATIONAL PEARL HARBOR REMEMBRANCE DAY

Every year on December 7th, National Pearl Harbor Remembrance Day is observed in the United States to remember and honor those who lost their lives. In Pearl Harbor, NPS and the U.S. Navy host a large commemoration ceremony, with survivors attending as special guests.

The USS *Arizona*, part of World War II Valor in the Pacific National Monument, is a place of great tragedy but also a place of great self-reflection. This site has served to promote peace and reconciliation between the United States and Japan in the years following World War II.

DIVE INTO HISTORY

Do you want to dive further into history? Reading this book is the first step to getting out there, exploring, and learning about how the past has shaped our present and may affect our future. Discover your family's World War II story. Talk to your parents, grandparents, and other extended family and ask questions. Seek out **veterans** in your community and visit memorials to get a better understanding of our nation's past.

Do you want to learn about other National Parks that preserve America's World War II history? World War II Valor in the Pacific National Monument is just one part of a much larger story. Out of 417 National Park Service units around the country, almost 40 are related to World War II history, and you can dive at over 60 of them. There are countless ways to explore America through our nation's national parks!

A young visitor, Landon Knestrick, meets his heroes, USS *Arizona* survivors Donald Stratton, Lauren Bruner, and Lou Conter (from left to right) on December 7, 2017.

Websites where you can learn more about these national parks:

World War II Valor in the Pacific National Monument
(this includes the USS *Arizona* Memorial):
http://www.nps.gov/valr

Recorded Live Dives on the USS *Arizona*:
https://www.nps.gov/valr/learn/live-dive.htm

World War II sites in the National Park Service:
https://www.nps.gov/subjects/worldwarii/visit.htm

Scuba diving in National Parks:
https://www.nps.gov/subjects/underwater/index.htm

PHOTO CREDITS

All photographs by Brett Seymour, NPS, with the exception of the following:
VI World War II Valor in the Pacific NM Archives; 7 NPS Photo; 10 Susanna Pershern, NPS; 16 NPS Submerged Resources Center Archives, 19 David Conlin, NPS, 25 World War II Valor in the Pacific NM Archives; 38 (top image) Naomi Blinick, NPS; 40 NPS Submerged Resources Center Archives; 41 Courtesy of Autodesk; 43 (bottom image) Naomi Blinick, NPS; 49 NPS SRC/WHOI/MITech ROV image, 58 Naomi Blinick, NPS ; 64 Naomi Blinick, NPS, 68 Naomi Blinick, NPS; 71 (middle image) Elyse Butler; 71 (bottom image) courtesy of Emily Pruett.

ABOUT THE AUTHOR

Naomi Blinick is an underwater photographer, marine biologist, NPS diver, and former member of the dive team at the USS *Arizona* Memorial. She produced the original version of *Beneath Pearl Harbor: USS Arizona* with underwater photographer Brett Seymour of the NPS Submerged Resources Center. After seeing the book's popularity with younger audiences, she was motivated to make a version for them. She hopes readers enjoy discovering what lies beneath Pearl Harbor and become enthusiasts and stewards for all the national park sites in the United States.

CONTRIBUTORS

Brett Seymour is the Deputy Chief of the U.S. National Park Service's Submerged Resources Center, based in Denver, Colorado. He has worked as a full-time underwater photographer with the NPS since 1994. Through his position he is able to bring many underwater historic sites to the public, including the USS *Arizona*.

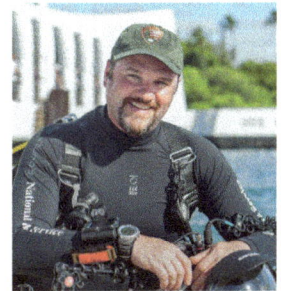

Emily Pruett is a former educational interpreter at World War II Valor in the Pacific and Cabrillo National Monuments. She is currently living in San Diego with her family. She loves U.S. history and was honored to be a part of the team that brought the live dives to reality and homes around the world. She hopes readers enjoy this book and are inspired to discover their family's World War II story.

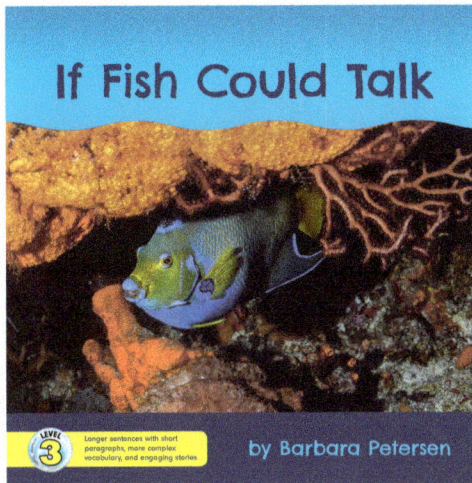

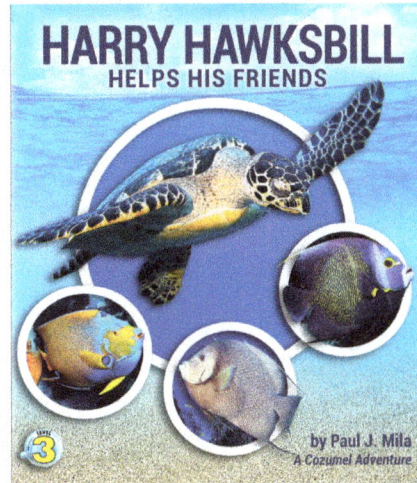

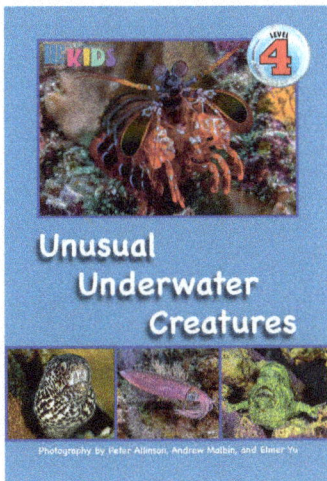

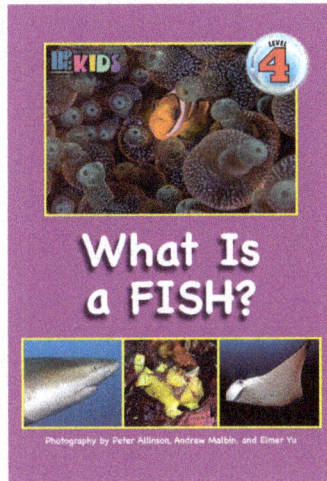

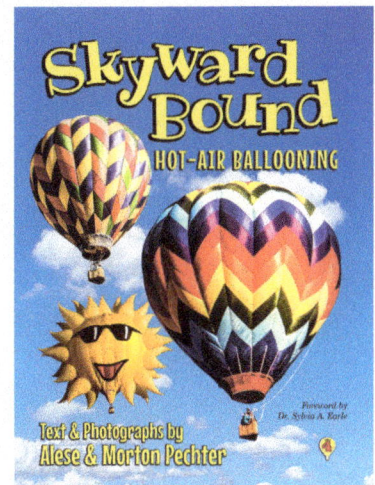

www.ingramcontent.com/pod-product-compliance
Lightning Source LLC
Chambersburg PA
CBHW041634040426
42447CB00020B/3484